HAVE YOU SEEN MY FATHER?

by
Judy Norris

A Division of Standard Publishing
Cincinnati, Ohio
40020

Library of Congress Catalog Card No. 74-28723

ISBN: 0-87239-030-6

**TO OUR CHILDREN
FRED, BECKY, AND NONA**

Loving as deeply as we loved them
taught us to reach for the hand of God.

CONTENTS

Who Is God?

Who is God? If you're a crossword puzzle addict, you've already learned that any time the instructions say, "An abstract being," "God" is the answer. Most of us have difficulty with abstracts. We want something concrete. We also want a personal God, so many of us build one to our own liking.

Some of us maintain the childish notion of God as a benevolent old gentleman, typical grandfather type, sitting on a pink cloud. This little man-made god cluck-clucks slightly at man's sins, but doesn't become upset. With this god, everyone goes to Heaven and lives happily ever after.

Still others see only a punishing malevolence, staring at the world to catch us in some misdeed. Of course, we have a tendency to believe he only dislikes the sins of our neighbors. Our sins are perfectly respectable, but he'll eventually punish all of those who distress or annoy us. Sometimes, however, we really are terribly afraid of this malevolent god ourselves and all our motivations come from a sense of fear of the hereafter.

But what is God really like? Jesus solved that problem for us for all time when He said, "He that hath seen me hath seen the Father" (John 14:9).

Will you look at Jesus with me?

Of Course, I Want to Heal You!

For God so loved the world, that he gave his only be-
gotten Son, that whosoever believeth in him should
not perish, but have everlasting life. For God sent not
his Son into the world to condemn the world; but that
the world through him might be saved.

—John 3:16, 17

How familiar our Scripture quotation is! Most of
us learned it as children. But a dear minister friend
named Estal Taylor made it come alive for me.
Estal always said, "For God so loved Estal Taylor."
Estal knew how to make the Word of God personal.
Yet, the thought of God's love in this often ugly
world presents a tremendous problem to the thinking Christian.

Leprosy is an ugly disease. Facial features frequently become bulbous and distorted. In later
stages, parts of the body drop off. People feared it
so in Jesus' day. I'm sure we still would if it were a
common ailment of our area.

In the eighth chapter of Matthew, we read the
story of a leper who came to Jesus. "If you want to,
you can heal me," he pled. Jesus' response was
immediate. "Of course, I want to heal you!"

It's very hard for us to comprehend the emotional
suffering of lepers in the first century. Being ill was
bad enough. Add to that complete ostracism from
all humanity except other lepers. Everywhere they
went, they were forced by law to cry, "Unclean!
Unclean!" To the sensitive, loving soul, how tortur-
ous this must have been. Men ran from them. Even
the sight of them produced gasps of horror.

Then Jesus came. Imagine the fear in the heart of this courageous leper. Does that sound like a contradiction? Fear quite often accompanies courage. In fact, wisdom and experience create fear which only singleness of purpose can overcome. The leper of our story was not only courageous, he was almost rude. His deeply wounded spirit cried out, perhaps bitterly, "If you want to, you can heal me!"

Religious leaders of his day would have chased the leper away, perhaps with an ugly retort. "How dare you talk to us, your superiors, this way? You forget your position!" They claimed to speak for God. They emphasized the letter of the law. They lived highly moral lives.

But the Son of God ignored the implied bitter challenge. He looked within. His heart reached out with compassion, understanding that humanity often screams in bitter anger while overcome with agony. "Of course, I want to heal you!"

In one of our early ministries, I became very fond of a young woman near my age in the congregation. We did a number of things together, especially while my husband was overseas as a chaplain. Finally one day she came to see me, obviously quite agitated.

"Have you ever thought what it might do to you to be seen with me all the time?"

"What's so earth shattering about being seen with you?"

From the depths of her soul, a story poured forth, a story I already knew. It was a tragic story of a rebellious adolescent, the youngest in a large family of children. Her parents were godly people. Her brothers and sisters led exemplary lives. But she became involved with some young people who were bad news. She found herself pregnant and had to tell her parents. After much discussion, a decision against marriage was reached. She also decided not to give her baby away.

Let's call her Anne, although that's not her name. Anne gave birth to a beautiful baby girl. With her baby in her arms, she walked down the aisle of that church and asked the congregation's forgiveness and understanding. They opened their hearts and lives both to her and to her child.

Not everyone else did though. Anne confided the problems she'd endured with men who considered her fair game after they knew her story. She told me how her little girl had been forced to bear insults. "You don't have any daddy!"

Anne's daughter died the year before we arrived at that church. As we talked that day, she told me she wasn't sorry about her daughter's death. "Her life would have been so difficult. All because of me!" She didn't cry. A broken heart can run completely out of tears.

I've pondered this many times through the years. We've lost track of Anne. We've often wanted to tell her what we feel she did for that congregation. Of all the churches we've served, that one had the finest spirit. Visitors often remarked, "We can feel the Spirit of God moving among the people here!" How much of that did Anne create? When I knew her, her Christian spirit fairly glowed for all to see. What about that repentant, heartbroken teenager who stood with her baby, pleading, "Forgive me! Accept and love my baby!" No bitterness! No recriminations! Most of the time when things like this happen, the church has failed that young person too. Could the love and confidence she showed in them have helped make that group of people into the type of folk we found there? Or were they already that way and she knew it? I don't know, but I do know she had complete faith that they, in God's love, would help heal her broken spirit and build her child's life. And they arose to the challenge!

Each of us bears in his soul some form of disfiguring leprosy. We know this deep in our own minds. But we often fear to confess it to God.

Perhaps we've timidly opened our hearts to people, only to be rejected. So, we go through life, in our subconscious minds, at least, crying, "Unclean! Unclean!" We may even feel that our only course of action is to maintain a relationship only with those we consider equally as leprous as ourselves. Our hearts weep in agony, "How can anyone love me, disfigured and ugly as I know I am inside?"

The beautiful response confronts us from the pages of God's Word. "I can! I can love you! What's more, I want to heal you. Throw out your preconceived notions. Knock down your walls of bitterness. Discard the masks you think you must wear. I love you! And, if you've seen me, you've seen the Father. He loves you too. Please, dear one, look!"

Have we the courage in the midst of our fears to respond?

Our Father God, we're searching. We know how desperately our leprosies of life need Your healing touch. Give us the faith for the long look through Jesus Christ, Your Son, amen.

How Small Your Faith Is!

But without faith it is impossible to please him: for he that cometh to God must believe that he is, and that he is a rewarder of them that diligently seek him.

—Hebrews 11:6

No one ever described Jesus as ordinary. His words and actions brought people to listen and see. His questions disturbed the finest minds of His day. One of His most outstanding characteristics lay in His refusal to be simperingly polite. Kind, yes. Compassionate, yes. But never politely insincere. He told it like it was!

In the eighth chapter of Matthew, we read a story about Jesus and His disciples on the Sea of Galilee. The pressures of the multitudes often forced Christ to retreat to the sea or the mountains. As He walked the dusty roads of Palestine, Jesus taught. He healed. He dealt with many problems of the human personality. Weariness racked His body as it does ours. It seems that following extremely stressful situations, He withdrew to some quiet spot. Our story involves such an incident.

After a long, tiring session, the little band of disciples boarded a fishing boat. They pushed out to sea. Exhaustion caused Jesus to fall asleep.

On the Sea of Galilee sudden storms strike without warning. Such a storm occurred while Jesus was sleeping. The Bible tells us waves were so high that they came up over the boat. Jesus must have been below somewhere, for He slept on.

Finally, the frightened disciples awakened Him. "Save us, Lord! We're about to die!"

I wonder how He looked at them. Was it with sadness, perhaps even pain? He said, "Why are you so afraid? How small your faith is!" Then He rebuked the wind and the waves and a peaceful calm descended upon the company. Some thoughtful folk questioned. "What kind of man is this? Even nature's forces obey Him!"

How like those disciples we are! We give our lives to Christ. Happiness radiates as we sense His nearness. Then some sudden storm breaks over the peaceful calm of our lives. We scream in terror "Lord, what's the matter? Are You asleep? We're about to die!"

One of the most outstanding Christians I've ever known was a humble little woman with a large family of children. We first became acquainted with her during the days of the depression. Her husband lost his job. She cleaned house for people in order to feed her children.

One day Mary (not her name) returned from work to find that her husband had sexually molested each of their children. My parents helped with medical care for the youngsters. She called the police and had her husband arrested.

In those days such a situation was practically unheard of. We didn't read stories like that regularly in newspapers and novels. Mary probably felt disgraced. But no one would have known. I can still remember her marching into the church Sunday mornings, Sunday evenings, and Wednesday evenings with those children scrubbed until they shone! Mary studied her Bible so earnestly that she even took notes on all the sermons and prayer meeting lessons.

One night our phone rang. It was Mary. "My little son has been hit by a car. I'm at the hospital alone. Could you come?" My parents went immediately. By morning, Mary's son was dead.

She got a little thinner, a little more careworn, but life must go on. She had the other children. I can still remember her saying, "God gives us no more burdens than we can bear. I'll see Joey in Heaven."

World War II came, and her older son was called to service. One of those crushing telegrams we all feared in those days came. "The War Department regrets to inform you . . ." Johnny was gone also!

Most of us would have screamed, "Why Lord? Why me?" But not Mary. "Life goes on. God is good. I'll know the reason some day."

Mary's daughters are beautiful people today, full of faith and vitality in living. Her grandchildren are outstanding, both in adjustment to life and in glorious Christian service. All because one little woman never let go of her faith even in times of tragedy.

We all experience storms in life. They may be physical illnesses, financial reverses. Perhaps our gale winds are emotional. Someone rejects or misunderstands us, someone very dear and important to us. Maybe we've set our hearts on certain goals. Suddenly it hits home that those goals may never be realized. As our ship of life rocks and reels, we cry in anguish, "What's going to happen to us?"

Calmly the answer comes, "Why are you so afraid? How small your faith is!" If we listen, the strength of His personality quiets ours.

An interesting sidelight to this Bible story lies in something that's never said. Jesus didn't pat those disciples on the head and say, "Don't worry, boys.

I'll see to it there's never another storm on the Sea of Galilee when you fellows are out there!"

That's what we'd like, isn't it? Wouldn't it be great if we could be assured that no more problems would ever come our way? Or would it?

When our son-in-law and daughter were living in the west, they took a little Blackfoot Indian boy as a foster child. Scooter was five years old. But he didn't run and play the way other children do. He wasn't even toilet-trained. Mostly he just sat. Why? Scooter had been diagnosed as retarded. Other foster parents had said, "Poor little thing! His muscles are weak! His mind is slow. We'll just take care of him."

Larry and Becky decided he should really live. So they made a game of exercising on the floor each day. His muscles strengthened. he developed coordination. Within a couple of weeks, he was toilet-trained. Close observation indicated defective hearing and sight. So Scooter was fitted with glasses and a hearing aid. Now he's in regular school. Which was best for Scooter? "Poor little thing!" Or "You can and you will!"

If we're wise enough to know the answer to that question, dare we believe our heavenly Father knows less? We cry out in our moments of weakness, "Oh God, why must I endure this? Remove it, Lord! Do it for me!"

But testing brings strength. Carrying anyone around makes him a cripple. Spiritual muscles need training too. Could it be that God says, "No," or "Wait," because any other answer would destroy us? The church is full of spiritually retarded Christians today because we run from difficulty.

When Jesus calmed that sea, the disciples marveled. "What kind of man is this?"

As we wonder at the wisdom of Christ, do we ask the same question? There's a very simple answer. He was God in the man. But, in order to see God, we must believe that He is.

Our gracious Father, we confess to the microscopic quality of our faith at times. We often question when we really need to trust. But we know how much You love us. Forgive our shallow, fainting spirits in Jesus' name, amen.

I'm Not Afraid
of the Rough Places

Yea, though I walk through the valley of the shadow of death, I will fear no evil: for thou art with me; thy rod and thy staff they comfort me. Thou preparest a table before me in the presence of mine enemies.

—Psalm 23:4, 5

The dangers in the territory of the Gadarenes frightened first-century people. In fact, the road through that area showed no dusty tracks of caravans or even individual travelers. Folk avoided the place like the plague. Why? Two fierce and angry men lived in the burial caves along the road.

Cemeteries are never happy places. But imagine the terror in the hearts of strangers when, suddenly, from the city of the dead, leaped two ferocious, unkempt men.

Can you visualize the disciples when Jesus insisted upon walking there? Peter probably said, "Master, don't you think we'd better go on the other side of the lake?" When Jesus maintained His course, how they must have muttered among themselves! It seems to me the Bible indicates they did a good bit of muttering about things they didn't understand. We're not much different, are we?

As the wild, demon-possessed men leaped out at the company, can you hear their comments? "We tried to tell Him! Now we're all going to die!"

The story in the eighth chapter of Matthew continues. The demons recognized the Son of God and begged to be cast into the herd of pigs feeding nearby. Jesus agreed. The herd of pigs rushed into the lake and drowned. A lot of pork chops were lost, but two men were saved. The community begged Jesus to go away. Perhaps they preferred pork chops to people.

Many thoughts arise from this story. One of the most interesting lies in Jesus' refusal to avoid the dangerous road. People had been going miles out of their way for years because of those tragically evil men. In essence, the Lord walked right up and forced an encounter. Perhaps that was His only reason for taking that road. He often exerted special effort to influence the heart of one believer. But, could His purpose have been two-fold?

Sometimes we fail to understand the abundant life Christ describes because we spend all our time hunting easy roads. Pockmarked highways frighten us. We crawl along at a snail's pace, tragically hampered by nameless fears.

Not once can you read where Jesus deserted the rough places for easy traveling. He knew that life lived to its fullest must involve pain and suffering. He knew each person must face difficulty. Only the one who dares to walk among the cruel, the demon-possessed, and the wicked can really understand and possess abundant life.

While we were serving a church in Indianapolis, my husband preached fairly regularly at the Indiana Women's Prison. Our work at our own church was very heavy. Bill preached three times every Sunday. On the months when we conducted services at the prison, that increased his Sunday services to four. Besides that, preaching the same sermon the same way was impossible. Many of the prisoners had very little education. Vocabularies were limited in some. Biblical knowledge was rare. So sermons that appealed to them demanded special time and attention.

In addition to the preaching, different prisoners requested his counsel on problems. He spent many hours trying to help those troubled women.

On one of his visits to the prison, Bill asked the warden why they didn't use more of the ministers.

"There are so many churches in Marion County. Caring for the prisoners wouldn't demand so much of just a few men if you'd pass the job around."

"But, Mr. Norris," replied the warden, "most ministers simply can't communicate with my girls. The prisoners disturb them and it shows." So we kept going.

I'm grateful for the experiences there. One of the women approached me one afternoon.

"I won't be here when you come again."

"Oh, are you being transferred?"

"No, I'm being paroled. Didn't you know I was a prisoner?"

"No, I thought you were one of the guards."

"I'm a trustie, Mrs. Norris, so I have a certain amount of freedom." Then her eyes searched mine. "Does it matter to you?"

"Not the slightest. I'm glad you're getting to go home. Are you excited?"

"Yes, but scared. I've been here so long. I killed my husband, Mrs. Norris. But I'm so thankful I came here. I found God and His forgiveness here." I've not heard from her again. I hope she found God and His love in the hearts of His people in some church on the outside.

We took our choirs out to the prison to sing for the

women. They enjoyed the music so much. But, when we took the little Cherub Choir, the tears really flowed. As they filed out of the services shaking our hands, many a tearstained, hardened countenance looked softer. Many a prisoner whispered, "I have a little one like that at home." Christ showed us that abundant life must be shared to be known. With whom should we share? Who more than the most troubled and confused of God's creation?

Our Master said so many remarkable things to us. One of them was, "You are to be perfect as your heavenly Father is perfect." I've heard so many discussions of this command. If we're honest, we know how imperfect we really are. So, is Christianity hopeless? No, for He also said, "If you've seen me, you've seen the Father." We can read of Him and learn about that perfect, abundant life. We can see His compassionate understanding of our difficulties. We can comprehend His willingness to face all our encounters with us. We know He's not afraid of the rough places.

No, Christianity is not hopeless, but it's not for the anemic and spineless. And its worth cannot be determined by the conflicts avoided.

Our Father God, give us the wisdom not to create foolish conflicts. But keep us from running from encounters that must be endured to build strength. When the occasion demands it, give us the courage to walk down that frightening road, knowing You're by our side. We pray in the name of that One who drew the accurate road map for our lives, amen.

Do You Hear Me Calling?

Now the names of the twelve apostles are these; The first Simon, who is called Peter, and Andrew his brother; James the son of Zebedee, and John his brother; Philip, and Bartholomew; Thomas, and Matthew the publican; James the son of Alphaeus, and ... Thaddaeus; Simon the Canaanite, and Judas Iscariot, who also betrayed him. These twelve Jesus sent forth.
—Matthew 10:2-5

As I write this, I'm sitting on the side of a hill at a women's retreat. It's an hour before my next group arrives for class. The steep hill keeps me from going down and returning again. So I'm spending an hour alone with God and His creation.

How beautifully the scenery stretches before me on the horizon! The quiet reaches out to enfold me. Occasionally a voice drifts up the hill. Once in a while a rollicking laugh penetrates my solitude. The pure, clear air soothes my troubled spirit. How easy it is to think in such a situation! How readily one worships!

Jesus often retired to spots like this. He prayed. He made the productive decisions of His life in just such secluded areas. Before the selection of His apostles, He spent an entire night away from the hustle and bustle of the crowds (Luke 6:12, 13).

The story of the selection of these men surprises us. Do your realize there wasn't a single professional clergyman in the lot? As far as we know, not one member of the little band was highly educated.

Peter, Andrew, James, and John were fishermen. Andrew, apparently, was the first of the twelve to believe in Jesus. He led his brother Peter to Jesus, but he was not one of the innermost circle himself. Each outstanding event in Christ's life included Peter, James, and John, but not Andrew necessarily.

Peter appears vacillating and fearful at times, especially at the time of Jesus' crucifixion. Even during Christ's earthly ministry, this man, whose life presents a study in contrasts, fluctuated from ardent supporter to gross misunderstanding of the Master's purposes. Jesus understood Peter, however. Loving him, weakness and all, Jesus knew Peter would eventually become a tower of strength and leadership.

James and John were the sons of Zebedee, a wealthy Galilean fisherman. Jesus called them "sons of thunder." On one occasion they suggested Jesus call down fire from Heaven to consume the Samaritans who refused to accept Him (Luke 9:51-56). James was the first apostle to meet a violent death for his faith. King Herod Agrippa had him beheaded.

John's metamorphosis seems to me the greatest of the apostles, although this point could be argued due to the great influence of the risen Lord upon all of them. From one of the sons of thunder, John became the great apostle of love. He followed Jesus to the foot of the cross. Not once did he desert his Lord. The care of Christ's mother fell on John. His writings are filled with pleading that Christians love one another.

The Bible tells us little of Philip. However, it was to him that Jesus said, "He that hath seen me hath seen the Father." He obviously had a very practical type of mind, longing to understand, but unable to preceive visionary approaches readily. Yet Jesus chose him.

The name Bartholomew is a bit confusing. Yet Matthew lists him as one of the twelve. "Bar" means "son," so this name actually means "son of Tolmai." Many believe he's the same man as Nathanael, for Nathanael is named in the Gospel of John and Bartholomew omitted. Scholars think John called him by his given name and Matthew by his father's name.

The name Thomas has come to signify doubt to us. This seems tragic to me. Jesus didn't condemn Thomas for wanting to see. Why should we? Jesus offered an opportunity for all types of minds and personalities to follow Him. Thomas exemplifies this. What great assurance we discover here! God, through Christ, allows us to be different, to reach out in our own way! Thomas needed proof. Jesus supplied it. But, He did say, "Blessed are they that have not seen, and yet have believed."

Matthew was one of the best educated of the apostles. One had to have some education to collect taxes and record them for the Roman government. That was Matthew's position. He, too, like John showed an amazing change of personality. Leaving all his wealth and position behind, he responded with his whole heart to Jesus' request, "Follow me,"

James, the son of Alpheus, is also listed with the apostles. Some think he was the Lord's cousin. He was called James the less, perhaps because he was smaller of stature or younger than James, the son of Zebedee.

Thaddeus is known also as Jude or Judas Thaddeus. Some places he's called Lebbeus. He, too, is thought to have been a close relative of Jesus. The Bible doesn't say much about him.

Little is known of Simon the Zealot or Canaanite. The sect known as Zealots adhered strictly to the Jewish law and advocated religious liberty during Roman rule by the force of arms if necessary. Even to belong to such a group, Simon would have been a bombastic, passionate man.

The Gospel writers remain pretty silent about Judas Iscariot except to identify him as the treasurer of the group and Christ's betrayer. At any rate, Judas committed suicide in despair over his actions. His life and death are true studies in tragedy.

Why go into detail about the lives of twelve men in such a short book? They were all so different. Yet the Lord loved and called each one. All but one served Him well, even to death.

We have a tendency to pour people into molds. God never did this! He created great diversity in our beautiful world. He also creates differences in personalities of people. He teaches, through His Son, that all these personalities may be effective and useful if tuned in on Him.

The tragic life of Judas Iscariot indicates that even God can't win everyone! One of Christ's most intimate followers failed the test. I personally believe Judas could have lived in the annals of history as a great Christian had he repented of his betrayal as Peter did of his denial. Jesus taught forgiveness as one of the essential ingredients of His message. He prayed for those who'd crucified Him. That forgiveness could have reached Judas also. But Judas couldn't forgive himself.

Jesus loved diversity in people. He called twelve very different men. They started a church that still stands almost two thousand years later. Millions know Him because of them.

He still calls today. He calls some of us to one career and some to another. We can "do our own thing" for Him.

Dear heavenly Father, we're so prone to criticize those who differ from us, or even to think ourselves unworthy if we can't do the same thing someone else is able to do. Lead us to an understanding that Christ calls each of us with our own personal weaknesses and strengths. We pray that You will help us to open our hearts and minds to Him that we may serve Him in our own special way. In Jesus' name, amen.

Why Struggle Alone?

Come unto me, all ye that labour and are heavy laden, and I will give you rest. Take my yoke upon you, and learn of me; for I am meek and lowly in heart: and ye shall find rest unto your souls. For my yoke is easy, and my burden is light. —Matthew 11:28-30

Human suffering has confounded the minds of men since the beginning of recorded history. It remains one of the greatest philosophical problems of our time. No one can solve this dilemma by reason, but some thoughts may help.

There's the long look. We have a tendency to glance right in front of us hurriedly as we rush through life. The here and now supersede all other thoughts. However, horizons exist that we neither see nor comprehend. When we remember the Christian hope—eternal joy, eternal life—any period of earthly trial is not the ultimate.

Still we question, "Why must the righteous suffer? Can a good God permit this?" The righteous (and who is completely righteous?) are still subject to the laws of nature. God's Word assures us this won't always be, but it is now. Therefore, illness and death are the lot of all humanity.

If this is true, of what value is our Christian faith? If our lot in life is the same as that of the nonbeliever, is Christianity worth it? Or should we sail through life doing our own selfish thing and taking care of number one? We hear, "Life's too short to be bothered with this or that." But life really isn't short at all. When it begins, it's eternal.

We're quoting Jesus at the beginning of this

chapter. Perhaps no more reassuring words for man's predicament have ever been written.

When I was a student at Butler University, I heard Dr. Bruce Kershner's statement at chapel. He looked at that group of aspiring young preachers and said, "Every time you arise to preach, you must remember that you're speaking to broken hearts." How did he know that? He learned it at the feet of Jesus. He also learned it through living, for he was an old man at the time of his chapel message.

Who isn't bone weary at times? And emotional exhaustion takes a far greater toll than physical exhaustion. Who hasn't yearned for solutions in human relations? Whose heart hasn't cried out in agony or torment over some loss, some misunderstanding? Our problems may take different forms, but primarily they're the same.

We had the privilege of spending a month in Germany in the summer of 1974. There we met two of the finest and most interesting people we've ever known.

Dina and Emil Luik live in Tuebingen, Germany, and belong to the little *Christliche Gemeinde* (Christian Fellowship or Church) there.

Emil fought in the German army in World War II. He stopped a French bullet. It was a head wound, a very severe one. The doctors thought working on him was a lost cause, but they finally did insert a metal plate in his head. However, the metal plate rusted and the surgeons operated a second time. Emil was reduced to the state of a vegetable. He neither responded nor appeared to know what was said to him. Convulsions racked his body.

About that time, the European Evangelistic Society began in America. The first man to go to Europe representing the society was Earl Stuckenbruck. Someone told Earl about Dina and Emil. He went to see them.

Dina and Emil had been nominal Christians for many years. However, church membership had meant very little. Dina was desperate for help in trying to aid and sustain her tragically ill husband. Through Earl's help, she found a personal relationship with Jesus Christ. A radiant faith blossomed, undergirding her in her hours of discouragement and fear.

What a happy ending those frightening years had! We talked and visited with a warm, fluent, intelligent Emil. He walks well. His conversation shows rational thought. His eyes glow with love and faith. He, too, found Christ and His sustaining help.

Dina and Emil now offer the same sort of sustenance to others in need. Dina conducts a *Kinderstunde* (Children's Hour) each Wednesday afternoon, teaching the children of the area about Christ. A number of the children belong to French soldiers stationed in the area. Ancient enmities lie buried. Christ's love heals the wounds. Heartbreak disappears as old hatreds melt in His all-encompassing love.

As a child I did not understand the Scripture, "Take my yoke upon you" (Matthew 11:29). Then I read and saw pictures of oxen yoked together doing tasks neither could have done alone. Was this what Jesus was trying to tell us? Was He using the customs of His day to show us what it really means to be a Christian? "I'm not too proud to be yoked to you. Problems too big to be solved alone we can handle together!"

So things really are different for the Christian. He suffers. He dies. But he does nothing alone. Jesus gave another promise. "Lo, I am with you alway, even unto the end of the world" (Matthew 28:20).

We recently attended a memorial service for a lovely young daughter of a minister friend. Kimberley was fifteen years old. Her battle with a fatal blood disease lasted for five long years. At the memorial service, the officiating minister read some of Kim's original poetry. Ideas far beyond her adolescent years were expressed. How deeply she thought. One might say, "What a waste!" But was it a waste? Her hospital room was a chapel. Her grace a benediction. Perhaps she did more for humanity in her fifteen years than most of us accomplish in a longer lifetime.

Struggling through life's crises alone becomes a sad commentary upon our spiritual depth when we truly read the words of Jesus. If we've seen Him, we've seen the Father. And Jesus promises rest unto our souls.

Our gracious heavenly Father, deliver us from the hurried-glance type of Christianity. Give us the upward look so that we may truly see You and know You through Jesus, Your Son, amen.

Will You Truly Humble Yourself?

Humble yourselves in the sight of the Lord, and he shall lift you up.   —James 4:10

Do you really want Christ to live in your life? Do you really want His healing power? How much?

The strangest story about Jesus appears in the fifteenth chapter of Matthew. Most people approaching Him were guaranteed a warm and courteous reception. But, as we read this story, the Lord seems almost rude.

A Canaanite woman ran after Jesus and His disciples as they walked in a region near Tyre and Sidon. "Have mercy upon me, Son of David," she cried. "My daughter is demon-possessed and needs help." Jesus acted as though He didn't hear her.

Finally the disciples intervened. "Send her away, Master! She keeps following and creating a terrible ruckus!"

Then the Lord told her He came to the Jews, not to people like her. But this time she prostrated herself at His feet begging for help.

Jesus said, "Why should I take food from children and give it to dogs?" Never flinching, she answered, "Even the dogs are allowed to eat the crumbs that fall from the children's table."

Jesus complimented the woman's great faith and healed her daughter. The Scripture says the girl was well from that moment.

This story has always bothered me. In our day of emphasis upon tolerance, the Lord's statements seem so blunt. In fact, they're almost insulting. To compare any race or nationality of human beings with dogs really throws us for a loss. We wouldn't think of saying anything like that. Jesus was, of all men, most loving! So why did He make this Canaanite woman crawl?

Jews had no dealings with Gentiles. In Jesus' day, no one would have been at all surprised had He continued to refuse to speak to the woman. In reading the story, you notice that the disciples didn't suggest He help the woman. They just wanted to get rid of her. This was the custom, particularly of the Jewish hierarchy. Jewish religious leaders didn't speak to women of their own families in public places. And a Gentile woman? No way! In fact, one of their biggest criticisms of Jesus lay in His association with publicans and sinners.

Was He catering to the prejudices of His hearers for some reason? What about the record of His talk with the Samaritan woman at the well? He went out of His way in an apparent effort to meet her and convert those of her village. The Jews hated Samaritans worst of all. No, Jesus never catered to prejudice in any form. He'd have been more popular with the Jewish hierarchy had He been willing to do that.

Yet, Jesus virtually forced this woman to bury every ounce of her natural human pride. He made her beg. She had to acknowledge the fact that in Jewish eyes she was a dog. Or perhaps even less than a treasured household pet.

Any time we see Jesus doing anything so completely out of character, we must search for reasons. Why did He treat this woman so? Why was this story included in the New Testament?

This unnamed Canaanite woman knew exactly what she wanted. Nothing deterred her from her desire to help her daughter. The Lord always read people's hearts. So we must assume that He knew His remarks would not drive her from Him. It follows that this incident had to be aimed toward His disciples and those of us who would come later. Was He saying, "Turn your hearts toward God. Don't let prejudice or insult turn you away! It doesn't matter what anyone says to you or thinks about you. Stay in there!"

In one of the churches we served, a family took a foster boy into their home. That's not too unusual. But the boy was black. He started attending all the church functions. I directed a youth choir. Everett began coming to rehearsals. He never failed us on Sunday morning; he was "Johnny-on-the-spot" at 8:15 for the first worship service when the youth choir sang.

All the young people liked Everett. His personality fairly glowed. He had some learning problems, for he'd never gone to school much. We loaned him some of our children's books. He even thrilled to fairy tales and legends, for he'd never heard them. He was in and out of our home just like all the rest.

Finally he came to see my husband all alone. "I want to be baptized, man. I really dig all this about Jesus. What do I do?" They spent a long time together. Everett impressed Bill with his questions and his sincerity.

The following Sunday morning Everett stepped out of the choir to confess his faith in Christ before that congregation. There was scarcely a dry eye among the young people. They loved him and seeing him take that stand was a mountaintop experience for them. He was baptized immediately. We thought it a tremendous gift to an all-white congregation. Everett said he'd like to use his life to promote race relations because he'd found such warmth and acceptance among our people.

Early the next morning our phone rang. The unidentified voice at the other end of the line said, "What does Mr. Norris mean by baptizing that nigger?"

"When Mr. Norris took his ordination vows, he didn't say, 'Lord, I'll try to win people if they belong to the right clubs and carry the right credit cards and are the right color!' He promised to spend his life winning the world to Jesus Christ."

"Well, maybe Mr. Norris can't help himself. But I'll never forgive that family that took that kid in! That nigger is ruining our church!"

"If one black boy can ruin a church, I doubt if we had much to start with!"

After some further conversation, we terminated our talk, agreeing to disagree, I guess. I never knew who the caller was.

No doubt Everett had met some of this negative thought among the church membership. At least, my caller told me much was present. Everett never mentioned it, however. obviously he took it in his stride. You see, Everett really "dug" Jesus! So did that Canaanite woman!

Then there's the matter of pride. My caller's problem was pride. In the course of the conversation that day, she declared lack of prejudice. "I don't hate niggers. I just want them kept in their place, that's all. They don't belong with me and mine!"

Can the Holy Spirit enter our hearts when they're filled to overflowing with ourselves? Most of our problems lie within. Spiritual progress is blocked more often by pride than by any other single thing. We want to protect our image instead of wanting to project God's image!

Another thought appears here, I believe. Jesus was saying, "When God appears silent, it doesn't mean He isn't listening." Maybe some lesson must be learned first. Don't give up! Wait for the mercy of God!

During World War II, Allied troops captured a German city. In cleaning out pockets of resistance, they found the following scrawled on the walls of a basement where frightened people had hidden from the Gestapo:

I believe in the sun even when it's not shining.
I believe in love even when I can't feel it.
I believe in God even when He's silent.

Another problem arises from the story of the Canaanite woman: Our definition of humility. Our society thinks of humility as a passive and submissive trait. That woman was anything but passive and submissive. She actually was very determined! Perhaps a great many of our Christian definitions need rethinking.

Do you really want Christ to live in your life? Do you really want His healing power? How much?

Our Father God, we confess to being our own worst enemies in all spiritual problems. Enter our hearts with the joy and fellowship of Your beautiful love through Jesus Christ, our Lord, amen.

Your Thoughts Are Too Small!

For what is a man profited, if he shall gain the whole world, and lose his own soul? or what shall a man give in exchange for his soul?   —Matthew 16:26

What do you value most? Where are your personal priorities?

Jesus tried again and again to make His disciples understand His true mission. But their eyes were dazzled by the glitter of earthly kingdoms.

Jesus talked of beauty of service. He pointed out the frustrations resulting from extreme legalism. He tried to make them see God through Him. But they continued to hold petty concepts of God! They insisted upon their own little self-interest schemes.

Finally, we read in the sixteenth chapter of Matthew of the Lord's attempts to prepare His little band for His death. He said, very plainly, "I'm going to be put to death and will rise again on the third day." Peter was furious. The Scripture tells us that he drew Jesus aside and said, "Now let's not have any more of this foolishness. This must not happen to you!"

Jesus scolded him. Very bluntly, He said, "You're thinking Satan's thoughts, not God's. Get away from me, Peter! You only understand the ways of men, not of God."

I once heard a man say, "God gave us two eyes, two ears, but only one mouth!" There's another saying, "Be sure your brain is in gear before putting your mouth into motion!" Isn't it sad that Peter's one mouth was in motion when he should have been using his eyes and ears instead? How much grief and disillusionment he might have avoided had he tuned in on Jesus' wavelength. For one thing, he might have caught that part about the resurrection.

As Jesus continued to teach the disciples, He showed the basic difference between the thoughts of men and the thoughts of God.

Men say, "If you don't get things for yourself, it's a cinch no one else is going to do it for you!"

Jesus said, "If any man will come after me, let him deny himself, and take up his cross, and follow me."

I once knew a woman who used this verse of Scripture often. No matter what happened to anyone, she'd say consolingly, "Well, honey, that's just your cross to bear!" One day she came through with her stock answer when one of the church teenagers complained about having fat legs!

How very shallow we all become at times! We sing about the old rugged cross. We wear fancy crosses around our necks and on our lapels. We speak glibly of the cross of Christ. But we gloss over the real teaching about personal crosses as though it weren't even there. We, like Peter, think the thoughts of men rather than of God.

But Jesus doesn't stop at all this talk about carrying crosses. He digs even deeper and comes up with a statement that boggles the worldly mind. "If you insist upon saving your life, you'll lose it. If you lose it in me, you'll save it!"

Now, in modern jargon, that doesn't make sense. It's a contradiction. There we go again, thinking the thoughts of men.

Ask any doctor who gets well quicker, the patient

who constantly tunes in on every little ache and pain or the patient who gets outside himself!

Ask any teacher who learns quicker, the pupil who's tied in knots inside about himself or the pupil who looks outside himself at his environment. In the field of special education, the learning disabilities are not necessarily intellectual. Many are emotional blocks.

Who's good company? The person who's all fussed up about himself, or the individual who also shows an interest in others?

Psychologically speaking, what Jesus said makes good practical sense. But spiritually, it's dynamite!

I lose myself in Jesus. So I get outside of me. My little hurts don't matter, for I'm living for Him. My little jealousies disappear, for He's the important one. My little animosities go down the drain, for He's in control, not I! I reach out in love, not because I'm all that great, but because He fills me with love. Talk about abundant living!

When this happens, pettiness leaves my soul and I can truly understand that things simply don't matter. For what would I give in exchange for my soul? What would I give in exchange for such spiritual abundance?

When we moved to Lancaster, Ohio, our son made friends with a little boy named Jimmy. Fred just couldn't wait for us to meet Jim. They seemed to be soul brothers from the very first.

Then we became acquainted with Jim's parents, Mickey and Van. The same thing happened to us with them. The relationship simply clicked right from the beginning. Mickey and Van were choice folk and we couldn't miss the fact. There was also a little son, David. He and our Becky fought a while and played a while. All in all, it was a happy time.

But Mickey and Van didn't go to church much. They'd both been reared in church but drifted away as so many young couples do. Fred and Jim fixed that. Soon Jim's family became regular attenders at our worship services and Sunday school.

Gradually they committed their lives more and more to Jesus Christ and His message. As the years progressed, Van became an elder. Mickey worked with the children. She sang in the choir. Christ and His church moved into front stage center in their minds and hearts.

We watched this family deepen as they all matured. Jim now has his M.D. degree and has served as a medical missionary in Africa. David is an ordained minister. Both young men possess unusual intelligence and unusual commitment.

You'd think giving two sons to God's service would be enough, wouldn't you? But it wasn't. Mickey and Van wanted to serve God in a special way themselves. So they sold their home and moved to a Bible college. They live in a mobile home on campus. Van works for the college, sharing his own special know-how. Mickey works there too. The financial sacrifice was large, but they say the spiritual rewards far outweigh the material losses.

What do you value most? Where are your personal priorities? Are your thoughts too small?

Our Father God, tune our minds and hearts in on You so that we won't major in minors. In Jesus' name, amen.

Why Can't We Stay
on the Mountain?

I will lift up mine eyes unto the hills, from whence cometh my help. My help cometh from the Lord, which made heaven and earth.   —Psalm 121:1, 2

Have you ever climbed a high mountain on a clear day? The air seems so fresh. Life somehow appears lovelier as we gaze out over God's beautiful world from a mountaintop. High above problems and troubles, removed from everything but beauty, we'd stay on our mountain aloof from the world.

One day Jesus took His three closest friends to the top of a mountain. As they looked upon Jesus, suddenly He appeared totally different. His face shone. His clothing glistened as diamonds in snow. Finally, Moses and Elijah stood by Him. Peter, James, and John recognized them. The glory of the moment overwhelmed James and John. They were silent. But Peter spoke. "Lord, if you want me to, I can build three tabernacles up here for you and Moses and Elijah." Jesus didn't answer. God did. "This is my beloved Son, in whom I am well pleased; hear ye him!" The glorious moment ended. The four of them descended the mountain.

Ecstasy had overwhelmed Peter on the mountain. In the midst of tremendous emotional feeling, he had the idea of building three tabernacles. The moment was inspired. Peter was sure his idea was inspired, also. But God said, "Listen to my Son!"

How often we, too, fly off on tangents, considering our emotional ideas inspired. No one minimizes the moments. But our instructions must still come from Christ, not from our emotional fervor.

At the foot of that mountain lay heartache and sin. On the top of the mountain stood Jesus. Not only was his beloved Master there, but perhaps something really clicked in Peter's mind. "Moses, the great lawgiver stands with Jesus. That gives him the sanction of law." Then he glanced at Elijah, the prophet. "That's it! Elijah wrote about the coming of the Savior. He knows Jesus is the Christ, the fulfillment of his prophecy. Wouldn't it be great to stay up here? What glorious conversations we could have. We'd be away from it all!"

God made short work of Peter's suggestion. He went immediately to the heart of the problem. "This is my Son. Listen to Him!"

Later the apostle Paul wrote, "The law was our schoolmaster to bring us unto Christ, that we might be justified by faith" (Galatians 3:24). Many New Testament passages assert Jesus' fulfillment of prophecy. But God's voice spoke on the mount. "Listen to my Son!"

God's Son commanded descent from the mountain into the valley of struggling humanity. Jesus always knew another mountain faced Him, one called Calvary. He knew that crowd at the foot of the mount of transfiguration would eventually spit on Him and crucify Him. But He left the glories of the mountain for the troubles of the valley. And God said, "Listen to Him!"

How strangely we twist Christianity sometimes. We make saints of those who withdraw from the world, taking vows of utter silence and aloofness. We pull our religion into our churches, carefully surrounding it with walls of brick and stone. "We mustn't let the world get in!" we cry. Does it occur to us that refusing to allow the world to get in might work in reverse? We don't let the message get out!

It's easy to build our little Christian ghettos. We see each other. We talk with each other. We love each other. Once in a while we admit someone else if he's just like us. Jesus said something about that. "What does it amount to if you love those who love you? The publicans do that!"

But Jesus descended the mountain—right into the midst of a bickering, complaining multitude. And God said, "Listen to Him!"

James A. Garfield was a Christian statesman. He climbed the ladder of political and social success in the United States from a poor farm in Ohio to the White House.

Mr. Garfield possessed many talents. Among them, history records a splendid gift of oratory. His voice is remembered as clear and musical, his thought processes brilliant and candid.

President Garfield's mother, Eliza Ballou Garfield, became a widow when he was just a toddler. She possessed deep Christian faith and instilled it in her children. James was the light of her life. He was not only her youngest child, but also her most talented. When he traveled as a Christian evangelist, how pleased and proud she was.

Then Mr. Garfield decided to enter politics. Biographers tell us his mother wept. She felt, I'm sure, that her beloved son was leaving his mountaintop of religious experience to enter a valley crammed with sin and temptation. Nevertheless, he went. And the highest office in the United States was his. He had a very short presidency, for he met an assassin's bullet four months after assuming office.

There are some thought-provoking stories from Mr. Garfield's life as President.

One Saturday a special meeting of his cabinet took place. Whatever they were discussing must have had high priority, for the cabinet members wanted to continue their discussions on Sunday morning. President Garfield objected, citing a previous commitment. One of the men was quite indignant. "What could be more important than the business of the United States?" Garfield quietly replied, "I have a meeting with my Lord around the Communion table." I don't know what the emergency meeting was all about, but history shows that the United States survived while the President worshiped God.

Although his mother worried about his exposure to the valleys of politics, Mr. Garfield had learned his lessons well. He knew he must have the mountaintops of worship in order to maintain equilibrium and stability in the valleys of performance of duty.

President Garfield had left the presidency of Hiram College to enter politics. But he never ceased to care about the young men who would come from educated circles to lead national thought. In a letter to President Hinsdale of Hiram College, President Garfield asked him to guard these young folk well. He suggested that education often divorces a man from the heart. In order to be a leader of men, one needs to retain the heart of a child while developing the mind and muscle of a man, the letter states.

We refresh our hearts with childish wonder on the mountain. But we build adult minds and muscle while working hard in our spiritual valleys.

Do you really want to know God? Get to know His Son. He walks on those mountains for inspiration and refreshment. But mostly He's down here among His people.

Our gracious Father, we love our mountaintops of glorious light. Give us enough of these to make us able to touch the multitudes with Your healing message. In Jesus' name, amen.

Who Is the Greatest?

But Jesus called them unto him, and said, Ye know that the princes of the Gentiles exercise dominion over them, and they that are great exercise authority upon them. But it shall not be so among you: but whosoever will be great among you, let him be your minister; and whosoever will be chief among you, let him be your servant.　　　　　—Matthew 20:25-27

What's your philosophy of life? "I'm committed to importance!" Or "It's important to be committed!"

One day some mothers brought their children to Jesus to be blessed. Women occupied a very unimportant position in those days. They weren't even counted when reports were made of attendance at various gatherings! Children were also expected to be seen and not heard.

The Lord was exhausted and the disciples knew it. So they tried to chase the women away. Jesus wouldn't allow it. "Let the children come unto me. Of such is the kingdom of Heaven." Weary as He was, He took the children and blessed them.

In the eighteenth chapter of Matthew, we find another account of the Master's attitude toward children. The disciples asked Him, "Who's the greatest in the kingdom?" No doubt they wanted Him to name one, or perhaps all, of them. But He set a child in their midst. "Unless you change your attitudes and become as little children, you won't even get into the kingdom!" That must have thrown them for a loss. But He added insult to injury. "The greatest in my kingdom will be the one who becomes as humble as this child!"

Remember the story of the night of the last supper? Jesus girded himself with a towel and insisted upon washing the disciples' feet. In those days, the lowliest servant in the household performed this task. No one traveled in air-conditioned cars; the people walked hot, dusty roads in open sandals. Jesus selected a nasty, stinky job to do.

Have you known folk who believe in footwashing today? Have you talked with those who were preparing to attend such a service? Feet are scrubbed almost raw to get ready. What a disgrace to be found with dirty feet at the footwashing! Thus it's not really a service at all. It's a ritual and we miss the point of Christ's gesture.

The disciples were so much like us. They longed for public attention. They found the concept of spiritual values almost impossible to understand. Jesus manifested unusual power. Of course, He'd use all that power to establish something great and magnificent. They'd be His cabinet, the members of the inner sanctum! Now His statements about humility and service as components of greatness undermined their power plans.

Very soon after the ascension of Jesus, the "who is greatest" question was revived. "My spiritual gift is greater than yours!" the early Christians asserted. "I speak in tongues more than you do!"

A few centuries after the establishment of the church, some leaders set the church up as a little carbon copy of the Roman Empire. Again battles raged over who would be the greatest. Wealth and worldly power replaced humility and service. Stratification of importance invaded the church for which Jesus died.

We're still at it today. I remember a church choir when I was in high school. Two women considered themselves leading sopranos in that choir. Each Sunday morning they'd push ahead to get what they considered the most prominent seat in the choir loft. The rest of us were forced to squeeze by to other chairs in the soprano section. Many times those two women became very angry with each other. I've often wondered if they ever thought about how they looked quarreling over the most important chair. What a satisfied look appeared on the winner's face, as dagger-glances of hatred marked the loser's face!

I remember going to a church were one man held eight prominent offices. The church grew and prospered. Attendance doubled, then tripled. That man always insisted he accepted all those positions because no one else would do them. But, with new folk yearning to serve God, he refused to give up even one. How he despised my husband when six of his jobs were finally given to other committed workers! He wasn't really doing the work required. No one can with that many positions. But the prestige felt good. Aren't we all a bit like that? I'm not speaking of an evil man. He was really a very fine one.

We've all known situations where a small group runs an entire congregation. They usually pursue one line or another. Either no one else is smart enough to do anything, or no one else is dedicated enough. Any threat to their position is met with verbal brickbats or behind-the-scenes insinuations of misconduct. Even if the congregation is at a complete standstill and they're doing nothing to change that, they'd rather let it die than be deposed. Fear of losing their stranglehold often keeps them from being able to share the work with others who just want to work beside them. Even ministers sometimes seem unable to rejoice with others more successful than they.

Years of work in churches have convinced me of the divinity of the church. We, with our pettiness, would have killed it long ago. But God planned it to live. "The gates of hell shall not prevail against it," Jesus declared. Not even the little private hells we create within the fellowship itself!

What's your philosophy of life? "I'm committed to importance!" Or, "It's important to be committed!" Jesus spoke for the Father. His teaching is very clear!

Our Father God, help us get ourselves out of the way. It's so very difficult. We pray for strength to submit our wills to Yours. In His name, amen.

Your Life Is Showing!

Whoso shall cause one of these little ones that believe on me to stumble, it is profitable for him that a great millstone should be hanged about his neck, and that he should be sunk in the depth of the sea. Woe unto the world because of occasions of stumbling! for it must needs be that the occasions come; but woe to that man through whom the occasion cometh!
—Matthew 18:6, 7, *American Standard Version*

Bill and I began our life together as youth workers in a church in Cleveland, Ohio. How we learned to love those children and teenagers! Some of them were very little younger than I, for I was only nineteen when we married. The responsibility seemed great. Bill was seven years older, much more mature in his thinking. So I left all the decisions to him, and it was mostly fun for me.

Among the children in that church there was a beautiful little girl named Jane Ellen, who was perhaps eight or nine. We planned a special outing for all the children. Jane Ellen was very excited and nervous about what to do. When her mother brought Jane Ellen to the church, she told me about their conversation. Mrs. Hamlin had said. "Now, Jane Ellen, are you sure you know just what you're supposed to do?" Happily Jane Ellen replied, "Oh, I don't need to know! I'll just watch Judy and do exactly what she does. She's so perfect!"

I've often wondered if Mrs. Hamlin were trying to impress me with my responsibilities. She was such a charming, gracious woman. Had she been wanting to make me see the nature of our work, she'd have done it in some thought-provoking manner like that. At any rate, if that's what she intended, it surely worked. Chills coursed up and down my spine. No one knew my imperfections better than I! Memories of the times I'd spoken thoughtlessly ran through my mind. Ill-chosen actions came back to haunt me. Losing my temper with very little reason reappeared in my consciousness! Jane Ellen probably will never know what her beautiful compliment did for me. I never worked blithely or thoughtlessly with young people again.

Jesus had quite a lot to say about children. He loved them dearly. The Gospels bring us accounts of His admiration for their simplicity, their utter lack of sham and hypocrisy.

Read again the Scripture at the beginning of this chapter. Serious contemplation of the words of Jesus removes any "take it or leave it" attitude about our influence on children and youth. No way can we believe that God smiles benignly and winks at our foolish or evil influences. No way can we claim our actions harm no one but ourselves. At least, this is true unless you think you'd do a good job of swimming at the bottom of a sea with a huge millstone around your neck!

Have you ever seen an old mill in motion? The millstone is gigantic! Watching a millstone grind meal is fascinating. But I certainly wouldn't want one around my neck, especially when someone throws me into a body of water!

Some people spend time asserting the right to individual courses of action. Much of this is good. However, no one has a right to his own way if that way injures others.

Remember when educators aimed at making all

children fit into a niche? All the niches were just alike. Literature for mothers accentuated development of the well-rounded child. It was not important for a child to excel. So what if he did make all C's with an A type mind? Just as long as he's well-rounded. Excellence is unimportant! What if a child loves peace, quiet, and seems naturally a loner? Get him involved! Don't let him sit and think! That's not well-rounded!

We're still carrying much of this into our child-rearing. Little League baseball! Colt football! Brownies! Girl Scouts! Campfire Girls! Boy Scouts! Y.M.C.A.! If you're not a joiner, you're simply out of it. Sometimes I wonder if anyone ever heard of a bunch of children who simply get together on a vacant lot to play ball. And do little girls ever devise their own playtime with dress-up and dolls?

One day our youngest child came home from school, flopped on the couch, and started to cry. "I have to go to Girl Scouts and then to Swim Team. Mommy, I'm so busy I don't even have time to be me anymore!"

She was about ten at the time and her words shocked me. "What have I been doing to this child?"

Nona had been the kind of child who sat on the ground and patiently watched ants or bugs during her pre-school years! I thought of her skipping happily through our backyard all alone, looking up at the sky. She was singing her own little homemade tune. "Thank You, God. Thank You for my great, big wonderful world!" That was when she was seven. Here was the same little girl at ten, a bowed-down, over-organized joiner!

So, I said, "OK. What do you want to quit doing?" We pared down her busy schedule to a routine she could live with and still be herself. Some very unhappy leaders warned me about possible results. But she's a young married college student today, happy and well-adjusted. She's not lazy. She's very much involved in both church and community. She's still not a joiner. She still needs some time to be herself. Don't we all?

Perhaps one of the ways we fail our children the most lies in the realm of this extreme busyness. Do you spend any time in meditation and prayer? Your children need this example for the times when they must assume responsibility for their own lives. Will they know how because of you? Or are you racing on a frantic treadmill? If I could roll back the years, one thing I'd change: I'd spend more time in quietness. I'd try harder to remember the quotation, "Be still, and know that I am God" (Psalm 46:10).

What's your home really like? If your children were asked for their opinion of what's most important to you, what would they say?

A few years ago I passed out a questionnaire to teenagers, asking them to name the issues of most importance to their parents. At the top of their list was plenty of money and education so that they could make a good living. Only one person named "relationship with God and Christ" as a parental top priority. These were the children of the elders and deacons in the church we were serving at the time. Now, I realize children often misinterpret their parents. But it doesn't do any good to have fine ideas unless they come through loud and clear to our children! Millstones, here we come!

Are your attitudes toward others kind and loving? So will your children be.

Is your vocabulary gentle and gracious or coarse and vulgar? So will your children be.

Do you have a genuine personal relationship with Jesus Christ so that He lives in you? Or is your religion superficial and shallow? Legalistic and condemning? Do you have roast beef for Sunday dinner? Or do you serve up roast elder, roast deacon, roast preacher, roast Sunday-school teacher?

Do you really know anything about the road map for Christian living, your Bible? How can you keep your family on the right road without a road map? Can you lay a road map on the car seat, never consult it, and still get to your destination? A Bible unopened on the coffee table doesn't help much either!

Mature Christians also bear great responsibility for new converts who are called "babes" in the Bible. Do you suppose Jesus also referred to them when He spoke of occasions of stumbling? Do new Christians feel the Spirit of God in you?

What do you think? Millstones? Or a Savior who says, "Inasmuch as you've done it unto one of the least of these, you've done it unto me!"

Dear heavenly Father, the responsibility for guidance of those who are younger in years or in faith weighs heavily upon us. We pray for Your help in deepening our faith and maturing our minds so that we may be stepping-stones for others to reach a radiant relationship with You through Jesus Christ, Your Son, amen.

Must I Forgive?

Forgive us our debts, as we forgive our debtors.
—Matthew 6:12

"Forgiveness." What do you think when you hear that word? If you were asked to define it, could you?

Jesus taught with stories. In the eighteenth chapter of Matthew, we read one of the most significant of these.

Peter, robust and rambunctious Peter, asked, "How many times must I forgive my brother? Seven times?"

Jesus replied, "No, seventy time seven."

I wonder what prompted the question, what hurt Peter might have sustained. Peter's personality probably led to many situations where forgiveness was needed. Peter couldn't have been easy to live with. His wild enthusiasms and impulsive involvement must have created episodes very hurtful to him. More sedate and withdrawn folk have trouble accepting people like Peter. So rejection surely played a part in his life.

Another characteristic of open-hearted souls like Peter lies in unwillingness to keep accounts. Judas might have done that. Even Matthew, with his bookkeeping experience as a tax collector, might have been able to tally up his insult count. But not Peter! Did Jesus have His tongue in His cheek when He said, "Seventy times seven?" Jesus knew Peter wouldn't keep track of four hundred and ninety forgiveness experiences and then refuse to forgive on the four hundred and ninety-first.

Then Jesus told a story. "The kingdom of Heaven is like," He began. How often He started His parables that way! How anxious He was for us to realize the true nature of God!

A king decided to check the accounts of his servants. He found one man who owed him millions of dollars. So the king demanded the money. The servant couldn't possibly pay. The king issued an order for that servant and his entire family to be sold as slaves. The servant fell on his knees pleading for more time. Feeling deep compassion for the man, the king forgave him and wiped the debt off the books.

The servant left his king's presence. As he returned home, he met another servant who owed him just a little money. The forgiven servant grabbed the other man, choking him, and demanding payment. The debtor pled for forgiveness, asking more time. But the forgiven servant had him thrown into jail until he could pay back the paltry sum.

Other members of the staff told the king about the incident. He was very angry. Sending for the hardhearted servant, he said, "I forgave you just because you asked me. You should have shown mercy for the other man as I showed mercy for you." He sent the servant to jail. Then Jesus warned, "That is what my Father will do to you if you don't forgive your brother from the depths of your heart."

Perhaps no other aspect of Christian character is more elusive than forgiveness. We often hear folk say, "I can forgive, but I can't forget." The mind that dwells upon injustice and wrong never truly forgives. Some of us keep all our pet insults and slights simmering on the back burner, ready to serve them up at the slightest provocation. The result is ugliness. Such souls can never be candidates for the kingdom of Heaven.

I once knew a woman whose heart was broken by her husband. A marriage of thirty-six years ended when he became interested and infatuated with another woman. His wife had built her entire life around his thoughts and desires. The shock and devastation of knowing he no longer wanted her was bad enough, but she genuinely felt utterly disgraced by even the thought of divorce.

I watched this dear woman run the gauntlet of emotion. I understood very little of what was happening at the time, for my life was very busy. My thoughts were upon my own family. I'm afraid I didn't comprehend her needs very well even when she sought my help. But, in retrospect, I realize she fought and won a great spiritual battle.

As her tired old heart began to give her great physical pain, she sent for her daughter. There were some personal things she wanted to discuss to make life easier for her children after the death she knew was imminent.

"I know it's hard for you children to respect your father. It's difficult to do the things for him that his old age might require you to do. If you don't want to help him for his sake, do it for mine. I would myself if I could."

I'd been a spectator in a major spiritual battle. She'd run the entire gamut of emotion, from grief to anger, from anger to bitterness, from bitterness to acceptance, from acceptance to forgiveness, from forgiveness to the true agape love of the New Testament. I really know about this. That woman was my mother.

Lack of forgiveness turns the church into a social club where members can be blackballed. Only those who meet our own particular standards feel welcome.

Many years ago in a church we served, someone suggested a young man as deacon. We knew him well. We'd been entertained in his home. As I helped this wife with dinner dishes one evening, she explained to me that her husband liked to put the children to bed. "He always gets on his knees with them and has prayer after their Bible story. He never had that kind of training. He was an agnostic when we met. Now he wants our children to know God as he's come to know Him."

But some of the older members of that church board protested his election as a deacon. "He was an agnostic once. He wasn't sure there was a God!"

The real problem was forgiveness. They couldn't forgive the questioning of a searching soul. Some church boards wouldn't admit the apostle Paul to membership if they had their way. After all, he persecuted Christians once.!

This story has a happy ending. The man is an elder today. His faith has remained serene and secure through much testing. His mind, still open and searching, reaches out to God.

Everyone knows deep hurt, for we've all experienced it. Everyone bears guilt for having injured others. So forgiveness holds a vital place in life, both in giving and receiving.

Can we truly forgive? Jesus considered forgiveness of paramount importance. This story isn't the only one demonstrating the emphasis He placed upon this aspect of our relationship to others. When the disciples asked Him to teach them to pray, the prayer He gave was very short. But it included a section on forgiveness. "Forgive us our debts, as we forgive our debtors." Our forgiveness, like that of the wicked servant, hinges upon our ability to forgive others! Reciting the model prayer as thoughtless ritual is dangerous. Praying it from the depths of our souls brings healing power.

Father, forgive us for our hard, unrelenting hearts. In Jesus' name, amen.

Do You Own Things, or Do They Own You?

Therefore I say unto you, Take no thought for your life, what ye shall eat, or what ye shall drink; nor yet for your body, what ye shall put on. Is not the life more than meat, and the body than raiment?—Matthew 6:25

What is important to you? Things or people? Your relationship to God? Material security? What do you really love?

In the nineteenth chapter of Matthew, the story is told of a young man who came to Jesus. He said, "Good Master, what must I do to be sure of eternal life?" Jesus asserted that God alone was good. Then He said, "Keep all the commandments. Love your fellowman as yourself." The young man protested. "But I've always done that!" Jesus looked at him lovingly and said, "Sell everything you possess. Give all the money to the poor. Follow me!" The young man turned away sadly, for he was very rich.

The disciples didn't understand. Jesus told them, "It's easier for a camel to get through the eye of a needle than for a rich man to get into Heaven." The little band registered astonishment, "Well, then, who in the world can?" Jesus assured them all things are possible with God.

How many preconceived notions do you have about this story? Those of us who consider ourselves threadbare love to gloat. "Aha! Those boys who have all that stuff I want will never make it to Heaven!" Heaving a sigh of jealous contentment, we slide back to rest on our laurels in our "poor but righteous" snobbery.

After the close of World War II, my husband returned to a church in a suburb of Portsmouth, Ohio. He'd served as an army chaplain. I thought I'd sacrificed a lot for God and country.

Willis Hale, a missionary who'd been a prisoner in the Philippines during the war, came to speak to our people. I was always nervous about entertaining in those days. Since I didn't know Mr. Hale at all, my case of nerves increased. I'd scrubbed until things shone, but much of our secondhand, scraped-together furniture looked pretty sad to me. Then the doorbell rang. Mr. Hale walked in. He looked around our modest home and said something in Filipino dialect. I asked, "What did you say?" "Rich man! Rich man!" he answered. "That's what my people would say about you!"

Suddenly this story of the rich young ruler meant more to me! I'd moved from the position of the "righteous poor" to the status of "rich." It all depended upon the life experience of the observer! How hard would it be for me to get through the gates of Heaven? As difficult as that camel and the needle's eye? He rocked my security even further as he told me about the suffering of the Filipino people during the war. As he described the plight of missionaries in internment camps, people whose only sin had been trying to serve God, my own little self-sacrifice bubble burst wide open!

Stories have a way of getting to us, don't they? Christ knew that. That's why He told so many. But somehow we manage to sit in the "righteous" position. Suppose we moved around and played various roles. This would help us appreciate the problems of other people.

Another thing Jesus told this young man. "Love your fellowman as you love yourself." The man asserted obedience to everything Christ said. But was he? Are we? Can we really love and live in luxury while others are hungry? Have we ever done anything sacrificial, completely sacrificial, in our entire lives?

After the young man turned his back—ever so sadly, but turned it nonetheless—on Jesus, the disciples protested. "Now look, Lord, this guy has it made. If he with all his success doesn't make Heaven, who can?"

Isn't this the way we think? Our son left a settled existence, a lovely home, an assured salary, to join one of our mission endeavors. At the time he decided to go, no one knew where the money was coming from to pay him. The reaction of a deacon in one of our churches characterized much American materialistic thought. "What's the matter with that fellow? He had all those things! He blew it!"

I heard Dr. Fred Craddock, a professor from Phillips University, speak recently. He made a statement I'll never forget. "I've no confidence in a man who won't grow rosebushes because you can't fry rose petals in hog grease!"

How many of us miss the beauty of abundant living because of materialistic thinking? How many of us have really turned our backs on God as the rich young ruler did? Deliberately? Or just without knowing it. Do you own things or do they own you?

Our Father God, give us the insight needed to value spiritual riches above material. In Jesus' name, amen.

What About Wasted Lives?

He hath shewed thee, O man, what is good; and what doth the Lord require of thee, but to do justly, and to love mercy, and to walk humbly with thy God?
—Micah 6:8

"What do you think about deathbed confessions?" How frequently this question arises in religious discussions.

Or we hear some Christian lamenting his late decision to accept Christ. "Oh, if I'd only done this sooner! I've wasted most of my life!"

Jesus told a story. "For the kingdom of Heaven is like," He began. We read this particular narrative in the twentieth chapter of Matthew. This account follows the story of the rich young ruler, appearing to be part of the same discussion.

Ancient Palestine must have had employment centers similar to such places in our modern American cities. Employers went there at harvesttime to engage workers by the day. So Jesus selected a familiar situation to explain God's relationship to people.

A landowner visited the marketplace to bargain with workers for a day's service. Offering each workman a denarius, he sent those who accepted this wage offer out to his vineyard.

Jesus didn't say why the employer returned to the marketplace at the third hour. Perhaps the grape harvest was greater than he'd expected. Maybe the workers he'd already hired had proved a bit slow or lazy. At any rate, he was hunting more people.

This time he mentioned no particular wage. He just assured them that he'd do whatever was right in paying them. The landowner repeated his visit to the marketplace at the sixth and ninth hours, promising the same thing to the idle workers.

Finally, at the eleventh hour, he returned and found other laborers standing around. He inquired, "Why are you still here?" "Because no one has hired us." "I'll hire you. Go to my vineyard," said the landowner.

When the day's work ended, the employer ordered his foreman to pay the employees, beginning with the last ones hired. The foreman gave each of these men a denarius. The first ones to be hired heard of it. "We'll probably get much more than that," they said. But each of them received a denarius also.

"Now, wait a minute! These men just worked one hour. How come they got the same amount we did? We worked all day!"

"I promised you a denarius for a day's work and you agreed to it. I'm not cheating you just because I choose to do the same thing for these men! Isn't that my business? It's my money! Are you envious because I'm generous?"

Today that landowner would have had a strike on his hands! At least, the employees probably would have formed a union with contract negotiations. From the human concept of fairness, the late workers were favored over the steady employees. But Jesus simply said, "So the last shall be first, and the first last."

Did you ever spend any time analyzing this story? What point was Jesus making?

How fortunate those early morning workers were to find a job immediately! When they entered the employment center, they probably were consumed with anxiety about whether or not they'd find a job paying good wages. Obviously the landowner's offer was a good one, for they snatched it up readily.

The question also arises as to the efficiency of their work. After all, the owner of the vineyard did make all those other trips to the marketplace. Could it be those laborers weren't exactly knocking themselves out to get the job done?

Another significant fact is that he made no specific promises to those hired later in the day. Could they have been so deeply grateful for anything he could give them that they made no requirements? They were paid the same wage. Perhaps they were so concerned with the late hour of their employment that they worked hard enough to make up for lost time! They might even have been equally·productive with the earlier employees.

One of the great tragedies of Christianity lies in the way those of us who've known nothing else seem to take its blessings for granted. We fool around through much of our lives with precious little attention being given to our work for God.

Then along comes a new convert. He may have been a rabble-rouser or an alcoholic. Perhaps he's a notoriously evil person who finally finds his place with God. We have a tendency to sit back and look suspiciously at such a person. "I'll bet that won't last! Nobody who lived this way can change at this late date!"

How it destroys our ego when one of these new converts grows so rapidly that he shows us up! When we're still griping around about small issues, he sails right by us in his spiritual life. His face assumes a radiance we've never known. Joy and peace flood his soul. Sitting on the sidelines, we complain, *"That's typical. He's become a fanatic!"*

I've known so many born-and-bred Christians who could use a little fanaticism. Perhaps that's a strong word! Yet so many Sunday-go-to-meeting Christians are just Sunday Christians and nothing more. While the world rapidly goes to Hell for want of Christian workers, most of us sit in our spacious churches wrapping our righteous robes around us to keep from becoming tainted! Perhaps our Lord has had to return to the employment center time after time hunting workers. I've seen few Christian callouses from hard work!

One of my favorite people is an alcoholic. Oh, he's a dry alcoholic. It's been many years since he's had a drink. For a long time, in spite of a dedicated praying mother, this man went from bar to bar. He even carried alcohol in his dinner bucket and drank all day on the job. He gambled away much of his salary. The prodigal son didn't have a thing on him.

Now, however, he's found God through His Son, Jesus Christ. When we first began our ministry with the church of which this man is a member, he went calling with Bill. As they went from house to house, several folk said, "Isn't that the man who was such a drunk? What happened to him?"

The years since his conversion have made our friend a great Bible student. How he loves God's

Word! We have seen him bring former drinking buddies to church. Prayer groups find him involved and witnessing.

However, when he was first suggested as an elder, someone protested. "That man used to be one of the town drunks. What will people think of our congregation?"

God doesn't think as we do, you know. He offers no labor contracts. Jesus proved that as He represented God to us. We might protest about eleventh-hour wages, but God operates the reward system and He pays them!

So what about deathbed confessions? I don't know, but God does. He understands the human heart. He also sees the hypocrisy in His people that keeps some folk from accepting Him sooner.

What about wasted lives? They're tragic, of course. But wasted lives can be recycled into God's kingdom. Sometimes eleventh-hour converts do more in one hour than some of the rest of us do in twelve!

Our Father God, erase judgmental opinions from our lives. Help us to rise above the plane of self-seeking into the realms of joyous acceptance of You and of our fellowmen. In Jesus' name, amen.

How Can the God of Love Be Angry?

And Jesus went into the temple of God, and cast out all them that sold and bought in the temple, and overthrew the tables of the moneychangers, and the seats of them that sold doves, and said unto them, It is written, My house shall be called the house of prayer; but ye have made it a den of thieves.

—Matthew 21:12, 13

Is anger a problem with you? What arouses your ire? Injustice? Hypocrisy? Personal injury? Lack of attention? Criticism? Social conditions? What drives you up a wall?

When I was young, I had enough temper for myself and half a dozen other people. Being the youngest in the family might have lit the spark. Teased about every thought and opinion! Not allowed to know family secrets for fear I might tell because I was "such a kid"! It's hard always to be low person on the family totem pole.

One of my teenage memories comes from a conversation with my mother. I was angry, perhaps for the umpteenth time. I can still see the weary look on Mama's face as I said, "I just think I'll give him a piece of my mind." Softly Mama replied, "If you keep that up long enough, you just may discover you won't have much left!"

At the time I found her statement a bit obtuse. I was so smart in those days that I thought Mama was clear out of it most of the time. Years of experience have taught me the truth of my mother's statement.

In churches we've served, there have been a few folk who prided themselves on giving others a piece of their minds. After years of practicing this little maneuver, we lose the ability to think. In its place lies only the art of flawsearching. "Practice make perfect." The old maxim even applies to the angry heart.

We search for insult. Naturally we find it. The anger reflex flies into action. We search for hidden meanings. Discovering what we're looking for, our angry muscles flex themselves and we're off and raving. I could go on and on. But if you're honestly self-evaluating, you know that I mean. We can practice this for years until we reach the point of no return. Reason and love no longer function in our lives. Every crisis or even tiny setback turns off our brains and sets off our anger.

Knowing the terrible lengths to which anger drives us, most of us fear this emotion. Yet anger occupies a very positive position in the human spirit. Without the ability to feel anger, the human personality loses some of its sparkle and verve. So what's the happy medium? Again we turn to our supreme example.

Jesus showed anger many times in His life. He became quite angry with the religious leaders of His day. Scathing criticisms poured from Him on occasion in regard to these men.

In the particular incident described in the Scripture at the beginning of this chapter, Jesus even took a whip and drove the salesmen and the moneychangers from the temple. What's more, He called them thieves!

People traveled many miles to Jerusalem to worship. It often was necessary for them to buy doves or animals after they arrived in order that they might have something for the sacrifices. Jewish settlements existed all over the ancient world. A temple currency was set up for this reason. Many times, in order to buy sacrifices, currency change was essential. So moneychangers became a convenience, or at times a necessity. However, many of the weary pilgrims failed to understand the monetary system. Many could neither read nor write. So the moneychangers cheated sincere worshipers miserably while pretending to serve God. Exorbitant prices were exacted for the sacrificial offerings. The whole thing was a travesty in the name of God.

Jesus had observed this on numerous occasions no doubt. The Bible doesn't state the specific reason why His anger flared in this instance. Perhaps He saw something especially flagrant. Anyway, the basis lay in love. He lashed out at the dishonesty involved. He zeroed in on the misuse of power. Each time we read of Jesus' anger, it relates to someone who's taking advantage of another. Most of the time the wrong appeared under the guise of religion.

As we search for answers about anger, again let us look at Jesus. He stood before the Sanhedrin accused of crimes He hadn't done. He stood in Pilate's court listening to a mob scream, "Crucify Him!" He hung upon a cross, bearing sins He'd not committed. Through all this, we find no flash of anger. We see pathos and suffering. We hear prayer and agonizing pleading with God, but no anger.

So perhaps anger itself isn't so wrong after all.

It's the way we use it. The moneychangers cheated people who didn't know the score. The religious hierarchy pretended to faith they didn't possess, thus misleading the people who looked up to them.

Jesus prayed for the crucifying mob, "Forgive them, Father. They don't know what they're doing." He could so easily have been angry. Instead He understood both His mission and their ignorance. Even that cry, "My God, my God, why hast thou forsaken me" seems to burst from agony, not from anger or rebellion. For it's soon followed by His committing His spirit to God.

What makes you angry? Most of us vent our anger upon those who mistreat us personally. When we fail to get proper respect, we're angry. When someone misrepresents us or gossips about us, our tempers flare. Quite often we remain pretty placid about big wrongs, especially if they happen to someone else. It's the little things that annoy us.

Anger remains a God-given emotion. But how we use it really matters. Peace at any price is never a Christian answer. Jesus loved deeply enough to get angry. So should we. However, we'd better be sure we're controlled by His Spirit and motivated by just causes when we do. We'd also better prepare ourselves for suffering when we exercise righteous wrath. When Jesus drove the moneychangers from the temple, the cross loomed rapidly on the horizon!

Our Father God, control us so completely that even our anger works for You, not against You. In Jesus' name, amen.

God Really Sees Inside Your Mind!

The Lord seeth not as man seeth; for man looketh on the outward appearance, but the Lord looketh on the heart. —1 Samuel 16:7

How many secrets do you possess? Do you wear a mask? Do you clothe your motives with sunshine and light? Are there actually cesspools of darkness in the inner recesses of your mind? What makes you tick?

Other human beings may not know. You may not even know yourself. But God does.

In the twenty-first chapter of Matthew, we find the story of a visit Jesus made to the temple. He was busy teaching the people when the chief priests and elders approached Him.

"Who said you could do these things? Where did you get your authority?"

The religious leaders of Christ's day sought constantly for a way to trap Him. No doubt the exact phrasing of this question had been carefully formulated. If He claimed God's authority, He could be prosecuted as a blasphemer. If He claimed Jewish legal authority, He could be prosecuted as a false witness. If He said, "I have no authority," the words would ruin Him with the people who listened. It looked as though they had Him.

But Jesus didn't react as they expected. "If you will answer a question for me, I'll tell you about my authority. Was John's baptism from Heaven or from men?"

I can just hear them suck in their breath. After all their careful planning too. "If we say it's from God, He'll ask why we didn't believe John. If we say John's baptism is from men, the people will hate us for they believed John to be a prophet." So they said, "We don't know the answer to your question." Jesus said, "I won't tell you about my authority either!"

You notice He didn't say He didn't know. He said, "I won't tell you, *either.*" In other words, He knew all the things they were thinking. He understood exactly how their minds worked. They hadn't fooled Him one bit in their attempts to spring a trap.

The religious leaders of Christ's day had replaced worship of the living God with a legal system and a shallow code of ethics. The result was a little man-made deity. They had enthroned their own intellects and wills in place of God and tried to rationalize all action by this process.

One of the most pitiful men we've ever known was a Unitarian Chaplain who served with my husband in World War II. They attended Chaplain School at Harvard University together. In the evenings, the men used to get together for what we'd call "rap sessions" today. They called them "bull sessions" then.

Every time something was mentioned that required faith rather than scientific knowledge, that young chaplain smiled knowingly and said, "Oh fellows, you just don't have enough education, or you couldn't believe that. I've advanced beyond that state!" Since Chaplaincy service required a graduate degree, most of the men to whom he spoke equaled him in education. They'd gone to different colleges and graduate schools, most of them more conservative than the ones he'd attended. Because he'd gone to one of the great eastern universities, he considered his education of much higher quality than theirs. He believed in love and that was all. Part of the time, He even questioned God's existence.

When the war in Europe ended, my husband's outfit was sent to the region of Marseille, France. There Bill again met this Unitarian Chaplain and they were requested to conduct services together. Each time, Bill's Unitarian friend wanted Bill to preach. "I'll make the announcements and lead the singing," he always insisted.

His personality had changed completely. Gone was all the bravado and superiority. Bill finally got him to preach one Sunday. All his eloquence and self-confidence were gone. He stammered awkwardly through a stilted bunch of platitudes.

Following the service, he broke down completely and cried as he talked with Bill. "Under combat conditions, I simply had nothing to give to my men! I had no assurance for myself, let alone for dying men. Oh, if I could only believe as you do!"

"Ask God's help and you can. Make the prayer, 'Lord, I believe; help thou mine unbelief' a part of your daily life."

"But I can't, Bill, don't you see? I once believed as a child. But those professors drained me of anything to live for, let alone to die with. Oh, if I could only believe as you do! They took everything out of me and left me nothing to take its place."

Religionists pretend to brilliance and knowledge no one can really possess sometimes. Teachers mislead students, filling them with doubts, making them unable to live abundantly. What's the difference between this and the Pharisees of old?

Those Pharisees didn't have to do any soulsearching about the effect they were having on anyone else. Didn't they have a law covering all overt behavior? They kept that law! And it's pretty simple to manufacture worthy reasons for all our actions if we just work at it long enough. It's even easier if we fence ourselves in and only associate with those who agree with us completely. Sound familiar?

The chief priests should have known Old Testament Scripture. Many Old Testament passages warn of the dangers of failing to see as God sees. When Samuel was searching the faces of Jesse's sons in order to anoint a king, he thought he knew whom to select. But God stopped him saying, "God sees not as man sees, for man looks at the outward appearance, but the Lord looks at the heart." Then God proceeded to select the most unlikely candidate of all—in man's sight, that is!

You'd think those religious leaders would have kept a regular heart cleaning in progress. Knowing what they knew of God's Word, why did they spend their time trying to trap Jesus? Why didn't they search their own souls?

When our son was a pre-schooler, he came home from play one day simply furious with his little friend, Troy. He launched into a long recital of Troy's evildoing which had precipitated a crisis in their friendship. I interrupted him right in the middle of the harangue. "Freddie, what did you do?" He looked at me with all the massive indignation a five year old can muster. Then he stamped his foot and said, "I don't want to think about what I did! I want to think about what he did!"

Children are at least honest about such negative emotions. But the sad thing is many adults still persist in similar reactions about either themselves or their families.

We see all the ugly and nasty motivations of others. We can note someone else's hypocrisy or insincerity from a block away. Maybe even from miles away. But somehow or other, we think we can brainwash every one else about ourselves. We even try to fool God! We, like the ancient Jewish leaders, manufacture our own little ineffective, myopic deities.

Jesus looked right into the minds of men. His spiritual vision pushed aside all pretense. His penetrating gaze swept away all superficial reasons and shallowness. Those who met Him stood before Him in utter nakedness of soul.

We still try to evade God's questions. How many secrets do you possess? Do you wear a mask? You might as well remove it. God really sees inside your mind.

Our Father God, give us the courage to do away with all our playacting and sham. Help us throw out our own little man-made deities, even the worship of our own intellects. Lead us into a close relationship with Your Son so that we won't need all these false supports for living. We long to be yoked to Jesus, but it's so hard to let go of ourselves and our pride. Keep us from evading Christ's questions as we walk in His way, amen.

My Father Abhors Hypocrisy!

Even so ye also outwardly appear righteous unto men,
but within ye are full of hypocrisy and iniquity.
—Matthew 23:28

Jesus often made people uncomfortable. Remember that woman at the Samaritan well? We read about her in the fourth chapter of John.

Jesus sent His disciples to get food for lunch. He waited by the well. A woman approached. Jesus spoke to her. No doubt she drew water during the hottest part of the day to avoid being snubbed by the other women. Most people did such difficult chores in the cool of the morning or evening. She probably disliked seeing anyone there, especially a Jew. When Jesus spoke to her, the New Testament fairly bristles.

"May I please have a drink?"

"Why ask me? You Jews think you're so much!" Jesus told her of the living water He came to bring, explaining its power to quench thirst permanently. She asked for the water and the Lord said, "Go get your husband."

"I don't have any," she replied.

"That's right! You've had five and the man you're living with now isn't your husband."

Now that was a conversation stopper, wasn't it? At least, it would have been for many but not for her. She'd been put down by experts. As their dialogue continued, Jesus told this woman He was the Messiah. She ran to bring everyone she knew to hear Him. That Samaritan woman helped bring salvation to her town.

How tragically accurate this story is about human nature. The Samaritan woman had been rejected so many times she probably wore callouses on her sensitivity. What was one more reminder of her sin? The self-righteous people of the town must have kept her thoroughly convinced of her low station in life. So her pride didn't get in the way of her learning of Christ. She didn't have any. She held membership in a despised nation. Even in that nation, she was on the bottom rung of the ladder. There simply was no way to go but up. So she listened. And Jesus rewarded her with kindness and salvation.

Knowledge of the history of that time arouses our compassion for the woman at the well. Any woman of that day who'd had five husbands had to be discarded that many times. The status of women forbade their divorcing men. As with so many people Jesus contacted, this woman must have felt utterly rejected and cast down. The fact that she argued at all showed the strength of her personality.

At the other end of the spectrum of humanity walked the scribes and Pharisees. They held high positions among the Jews. They could recite the law. Often they wore parts of it on their foreheads. Their unblemished rectitude fairly gleamed for all to see.

What a strange Savior we worship! Let's be logical. Shouldn't Jesus have condemned the woman and praised the scribes and Pharisees? Why didn't He?

The Samaritan woman obviously longed for something beyond herself to help her with her tragic life. But the religious leaders had it made.

They knew so much. They were so pious. They had ways of doing things, ways they considered undeniably right. "My father did it this way before me. Who's this young upstart who's trying to change things? After all, we had a religion when He came, and we'll have one when He's gone!"

The most ego-shattering phrases in the entire New Testament came from the mouth of Jesus as He encountered the religionists of His day.

"You won't enter the kingdom of Heaven and you're keeping others out! You cheat widows even while you're making big long prayers. You mislead people so that you make them sons of Hell like yourself! You tithe, but you show no mercy or love. You strain gnats and swallow camels." Then to top it all off, "You're like tombs. You look great on the outside, but you're dead rotten within."

When someone makes us uncomfortable with his teachings, we have just three courses of action. We may listen, learn, and accept. That's what the Samaritan woman did. We may walk away in order to avoid a decision. The rich young ruler did that, and it was a decision whether he thought so or not. Or we may try to destroy the person who annoys us. That's what the scribes and Pharisees did.

Hypocrisy probably invades the realm of Christianity more than any other single problem. We become upset or disturbed by either a real or fancied insult. Our subconscious minds know exactly what we're doing. We're wiping out the thing that annoys. But our conscious minds search for beautiful, ethical reasons for our decisions. So our souls dry up. Our consciences become seared and hardened. Time runs out, for we become incapable of seeing our own needs. We even shut out God. We bask in the sunlight of our own egos. As Jesus said of the Pharisee, we pray to ourselves so that others might see.

A number of years ago we knew two couples who belonged to the same Sunday-school class in a big city church. The daughter of one couple was a good friend of mine. The entire congregation was shocked one day by the news that my friend's mother had deserted her husband and children for the other man.

Naturally my friend was crushed. It was particularly difficult for her because she herself was getting married in just a matter of weeks.

I don't know what really happened. I do know that my friend's mother and the other man returned to town. He asked his wife's forgiveness and she took him back. My friend's father told her mother he wanted no part of her anymore and to get lost.

After much pleading on the part of my girl friend, her parents agreed to come to her wedding together. They buried the hatchet long enough to try to give their daughter a beautiful wedding day.

Following the ceremony, the wedding party formed a receiving line in the vestibule of the church. As folk left the church, I noticed a woman approach that line. When she reached the mother of the bride, she very carefully turned her back. She greeted the father effusively—a man with the spiritual sin of an unforgiving heart. But she refused even a kind word to a woman who'd committed a physical sin. Is there really a difference?

Could my friend's mother have been driven to the arms of another man by the attitudes of a cold, unrelenting, and unforgiving husband? Was her sin greater than his? Society might have said so, but does God?

Could it be possible that self-righteousness heads the list of deadly sins?

O gracious Father, keep us from the terrible falseness of self-righteousness. Help us to develop a healthy self-respect, coupled with humility and love for others. In Jesus' name, amen.

My Father Longs to Help You!

O Jerusalem, Jerusalem ... how often would I have gathered thy children together, as a hen doth gather her brood under her wings, and ye would not!
—Luke 13:34

Have you ever wondered why God allows certain things to happen? Why doesn't He simply wipe some individuals off the earth? Is free will good or bad? What would you do if you were God?

The Old Testament tells of God's anger. The writers of the ancient scrolls even record the fact that God repented of ever having made man. Yet all the way through the Bible, the thread of love ties all things together.

The idyllic garden of man's beginnings crashed down around his head as he defied God. Many of us were taught about God's wrath as we learned the story of Adam and Eve. As a child, I had visions of a fifteen-foot giant with flashingly angry eyes pointing His finger to the garden exit. Doing so many naughty things myself didn't help me a bit. My little body trembled as I looked at pictures of Adam and Eve huddled in each other's arms as they walked out to face the unknown. No Sunday-school teacher ever impressed me with the love of God exemplified in His clothing them warmly before they left. No one ever made me understand God's love for them in not wanting them to live forever in a state of sin. Perhaps I couldn't have comprehended such depth. But I believe even parental discipline would have been easier to rationalize had someone tried.

God's love comes through in so many Old Testament stories. Remember Abraham's pleading with God to save the cities of the plain? God would have spared all of them for just a few righteous people.

Joseph is one of my favorite Old Testament characters. God didn't protect Joseph from his envious brothers. But He did go with Joseph on his trip as a slave into Egypt. He did save Joseph's life and lead him into paths of greatness. Read the story of Joseph in the book of Genesis. No more thrilling story exists in all literature.

Are you familiar with the life story of King David? Joseph seems to have led an exemplary life. No sin is recorded for Joseph. But not so with David. Read about David, starting in 1 Samuel 16. David sinned greatly with Bathsheba. He even added virtual murder to adultery. Yet God loved him and forgave him. David was severely punished. The little son of their adulterous union died. But David bowed before God in humble repentance and found the forgiveness he sought.

God sent His prophets to His chosen people. They ridiculed and stoned the prophets. They either disobeyed His laws or turned them around to strangle the little people instead of helping them.

Finally God sent His Son. Are you really well acquainted with the Bible? Have you read descriptions of Heaven? No sin. No sorrow. No death. No sickness. Joy! Beauty! Laughter! Love! Jesus left all that to don human skin!

To our finite minds, this seems incomprehensible. We're so materialistic in our thinking. If I'd been God, I'd have sent my only son to a palace.

Jesus came to a stable. I'd have waded right in with both fists flying when people mistreated Him! I'd have blasted the whole depraved lot off the face of the earth when they crucified Him! In fact, long before time for Him to come, I'd have washed my hands of all mankind, I think. Aren't you glad I'm not God?

All through the life of Christ, He did all these incomprehensible things. When He said, "The Sabbath was made for man and not man for the Sabbath," those Jewish leaders practically climbed walls. When He said to that tragic woman caught in adultery, "Neither do I condemn thee: go, and sin no more," He pulled the rug right out from under all their nice little pat rules. They really believed they were justified in stoning her. "Let him who is without sin cast the first stone" was a frightening concept. Cut-and-dried solutions were so much simpler.

"Love your enemies . . . and pray for them which despitefully use you, and persecute you" was downright scary. It still is for us today. After two thousand years almost no one does that, you know.

There are so many things like this in the life of Christ. But perhaps one of the most poignant is found in the Scripture quotation at the beginning of this chapter. One of the Gospel writers tells us He sat on the mountain overlooking the great city of Jerusalem. Jerusalem represented God to the Jews. The magnificent temple stood there. The history of their people was inextricably tied to Jerusalem. But Jesus was weeping.

The Lord looked at that great sinful city and said, "Your entire history reeks with sins against God. I want to help you, but you won't let me."

If I were God, I might make puppets of men to protect both them and my beautiful world. But He didn't. So the choice is ours. As Christ looks at our homes, our cities, what does He say? If you've seen Him, you've seen God. So we know God longs to help us. But the choice is ours.

Dear heavenly Father, we know we are what we choose to be. Our prayer today is that our choices may be guided by You. We long for solace in the shadow of Your wings. Help us to find sweet peace there, in Jesus' name, amen.

Can't You Watch With Me
for One Hour?

And he cometh unto the disciples, and findeth them
asleep, and saith unto Peter, What, could ye not watch
with me one hour? Watch and pray, that ye enter not
into temptation: the spirit indeed is willing, but the
flesh is weak.   —Matthew 26:40, 41

The impact of Gethsemane can scarcely be felt
from one Gospel account. Matthew 26 and Mark 14
tell the same story. Luke becomes even more de-
scriptive. In Luke 22:44 we read, "And being in an
agony he prayed more earnestly: and his sweat
was as it were great drops of blood falling down to
the ground." Have you ever known such despair?

What about those disciples? Did they really love
Him? Did they really care that He was suffering so?
Of course they did. Both Matthew and Mark quote
Jesus as saying their spirits were willing. The flesh
was weak!

Isn't that the story of our lives? I know very few
people who find it impossible to love Jesus. Kindness reaches out to us from the biographical
sketches of Him in Holy Writ. His love enfolds us.
His empathy surrounds us. His blameless life im-
presses us. His suffering distresses us. Yes, loving
Him is easy. It's the watchful waiting that's hard.

At the beginning of my sophomore year in college, I rode a bus all night from Cleveland, Ohio, to
Indianapolis, Indiana, to enter Butler University. I
dozed some, of course. But really deep sleep
eluded me as other passengers laughed and

talked. Each stop created more wakefulness. Finally I arrived in Indianapolis about nine o'clock on a Sunday morning.

I loved O.A. Trinkle, a minister in Indianapolis. The Trinkles and my parents had been friends for many years. I asked direction and made my way to the church.

I'll never forget the misery of that morning. I'm sure Pappy Trinkle preached a fine sermon. I loved and respected him as a man. But I couldn't stay awake. I pinched myself. I tried uncomfortable positions. But the sleep that wouldn't come all night wouldn't go away that morning. In additon to that, I'm a front seater! I dislike the backseats of a church. So there I sat right in front of dear Mr. Trinkle snoozing away! The whole thing upset me so badly I never attended another worship service at that church. I know just how those apostles felt. My exhausted body simply refused to respond to the commands of my mind and spirit.

We're all a bit like that, aren't we? We hear an excellent, inspiring sermon and we tell ourselves, "I'm going to get more involved in Christianity!" All week long, resolution runs pretty high. Then Saturday night comes. Someone suggests a party. Away we go and the wee small hours find us partying or just getting into bed. Time to get up arrives. The alarm goes off. "Oh, I'm just too tired to make it today! After all, Sunday's the only day I have to sleep!"

"Can't you watch with me for one hour?"

The church organizes a prayer group. The minister urges participation. "It will just be an hour long.

We'll study the Bible and pray for others." We resolve to go. But it alters our routine. This must be done. We're expected at that meeting. Our card club or sorority meets at the same time. So the prayer group goes on without us. "We'd love to, you understand. But we're so busy!"

"Can't you watch with me for one hour?"

The church needs youth workers for the Sunday evening groups or teachers for the Sunday school. The minister or superintendent approaches us. "We'd really like to help. But we don't want to tie ourselves down to be there every Sunday and pre-- pare something each week. Maybe next year!"

"Can't you watch with me for one hour?"

The choir needs singers. We used to sing. Someone tells the choir director and he calls to ask our help.

"Oh, I know you're in a terrible bind. But I don't know whether I could promise to attend rehearsals every week or not. I'm so busy."

"Well, we'll see." Choir practice night comes and goes and we don't find the time.

"Can't you watch with me for one hour?"

Tragedies pile upon tragedies as we rush to and from busily doing little of value. While the church sleeps, our lukewarm commitment sends our youth to hunt for other more meaningful answers to living. They turn to gurus, eastern meditation cults, all sorts of isms and panaceas. When we open our eyes just slightly, we ourselves consult horoscopes and mind readers. I wonder. Does the suffering

Savior still sweat drops of blood over our persecution and neglect?

Suppose the apostles had spent their time praying as Jesus asked. Would Peter have denied knowing Jesus, or would he have had the strength to go through the trial with his Lord? Would the little band have dispersed to go fishing, or would they have remembered Christ's teaching about His resurrection? Could the hours of gloom and depression have become hours of joyful waiting? We'll never know, will we? They didn't watch that one hour! And while they slept, the betrayer and his mob arrived to destroy the Person they held most dear!

If God were only a God of justice, that motley crew of tired men would have met condemnation. Instead, Christ said, "The spirit indeed is willing, but the flesh is weak."

We could leave this right here. As one popular song tells us that God will always forgive no matter how much we grieve Him, we could lie! The Bible says His Spirit won't always strive with us. After all, those apostles spent ten days in a prayer meeting after Christ's ascension and went out to turn the world upside down! They didn't stay asleep!

"Can't you watch with me for one hour?"

Our Father God, we're busy about so many things that we exhaust ourselves doing nothing. Lead us to the right use of our limited energy. Help us to put first things first. Show us how to redeem our time for our Redeemer. In His name, amen.

Father, Forgive Them

And when they were come to the place, which is called Calvary, there they crucified him . . . Then said Jesus, Father, forgive them; for they know not what they do.
—Luke 23:33, 34

Pathos cries out to us from the Gospels as we read the story of Jesus' betrayal and crucifixion. We cringe at the thought of the terrible pain of the nails in His hands and feet. We shudder with horror at the sound of His cross dropping into the hole prepared for it. We're inclined to think, "What was the matter with those people? What had He done? He healed the sick. He comforted the troubled. He raised the dead. The lowest in the social caste system found understanding and solace in His life and message. How could those people torture Him so?"

Crucifixion occupies a very special spot in the history of man's inhumanity to man. Perhaps no more barbaric means of execution ever existed. Many victims hung for days before death claimed them. Usually the Romans reserved this method of execution for the lowest of their criminals. Jesus certainly did not qualify as the criminal type. But He frightened the authorities. His rare powers! His great appeal to the masses! His refusal to be a puppet in the hands of the Jewish leaders! He wasn't wicked, but He was alarming. No one met Him and remained the same. If people were to exist in their own special little ruts, He had to go!

How those religious leaders must have gloated when they finally got their way and He was led off to die. "Now that we've gotten rid of this fellow, we can get everything under control again. The trouble with the common man is that he believes impostors like this. But we all knew better and the crowd will come around. After all, they're used to doing as we say. And it's best for them! This man couldn't have come from God. *We'd* have known!"

I wonder what they thought when He prayed for them after all they'd done: "Father, forgive them; for they do not know what they are doing." When He'd said, "Pray for your enemies," it hadn't impressed them much. They didn't think that way. They probably considered it just a line to make Him appear pious to the multitude. But, let's face it, times for impressing anyone were gone. The man was dying. This was for real! And He, personally, was praying for them, His enemies. Could they have been wrong? Were they crucifying God? Do you suppose any of them wondered?

Perhaps no more definitive statement of the personality of God appears in the entire Bible. Suppose you'd been denied by a dear friend, deserted by almost everyone you knew well, and betrayed by one of your closest associates. Imagine having been beaten until your flesh was raw. Think of having no sleep while being unfairly and illegally tried for wrongs you hadn't committed. Suppose you'd been laughed at, spit upon, and ridiculed. Then after condemnation you never deserved, soldiers had tried to make you carry a cross on your bruised and bleeding back. Can you conceive of having great spikes driven into your hands and feet? Could you pray for the stupid and evil people who did all this?

If we're honest, we must admit that most of us could think of nothing but ourselves in the midst of such physical and emotional torment. Should we consider our oppressors at all, it would surely be with revulsion and anger. Pity? No way! Prayer of intercession for such depraved humanity? Never! How could anyone do it?

Just "anyone" couldn't! But Jesus could. Jesus was God in human skin. God could!

This prayer of Christ does amazing things for me. It says, "I love you." In this prayer, Jesus insists, "I can continue to love and understand you even at your very worst." I need that in my life. Don't you?

Very few of us will ever be called upon to bear such extreme physical suffering as crucifixion. Even those who linger for months with some sort of malignancy or other devastating disease can count upon the wonderful methods of sedation devised by modern science. However, most of us experience rejection and emotional wounds. Is this all part of what Christ came to display?

No one would have blamed Jesus had He lashed out in anger at His tormentors. But He didn't. We could all understand had He pleaded with God to destroy all of them in one tremendous flash of power. But He didn't. Why not?

God had tried and tried with His supreme creation, man. When man enjoyed the closest of personal walks with God in the garden, all it took was the temptation of forbidden fruit to create separation. Prophets, priests, kings, the great lawgiver had all come and gone. Still man refused to understand. So the supreme sacrifice was made and the Perfect Example sent! Jesus came, knowing the cross would be there!

"Father, forgive them, for they don't know what they're doing" carries the deepest emphasis upon human relations. "Love your enemies . . . pray for them which despitefully use you, and persecute you." He didn't just teach it. He lived it!

Isn't it great to see the forgiveness of God in the life of Jesus? I need that. Don't you?

Our Father God, we praise You for Your Son. We thank You for His perfect example in relationships both with You and with men. Give us the depth of commitment that enables us to understand and forgive others. In His name, amen.

No Force Holds God!

Truly this was the Son of God. . . . And, behold, there was a great earthquake: for the angel of the Lord descended from heaven, and came and rolled back the stone from the door, and sat upon it. . . . And Jesus came and spake unto them, saying, All power is given unto me in heaven and in earth.

—Matthew 27:54; 28:2, 18

Outlined against a leaden sky stood three crosses. In the center hung Jesus of Nazareth. His only sin had been representing God so completely that mediocre men couldn't understand Him. Now the strength of the Roman Empire had moved into the picture. He was dead. Materialistic forces had won. Those tender, compassionate hands, offering love and healing to so many, were quiet now. The voice that had thrilled multitudes with teachings and thoughts far above the knowledge of men seemed forever stilled. Those small-minded, self-seeking religious leaders who'd stirred up the unthinking mob had finally achieved what they set out to do. Still they were uneasy.

God's wrath split the earth and sky. The temple veil was torn in two. In spite of all these frightening experiences, one lone centurion at the foot of the cross seems to have been the only one declaring Christ's divinity.

Loving hands lifted the Lord's broken body down from the cross. Joseph of Arimathea and Nicodemus wrapped Him in linen cloths and laid Him in Joseph's new tomb. How they must have grieved over the travesty called justice their associates in the Sanhedrin had perpetrated! At least His suffering was over.

The Jewish leaders still worried. "Suppose His followers steal His body and pretend He arose. We must have guards and a seal!"

So they went to Pilate, who must have been very weary of them and their underhanded dealings. "Why couldn't the emperor have made me governor somewhere else? This bunch of unruly Jews could drive a man mad!" must have coursed through his mind. But he gave them guards, a huge stone, and a seal over the grave entrance. Finally, they returned home satisfied that nothing could rock their pious little boats again.

But the morning of the first day of the week brought a great earthquake. An angel rolled away the stone and sat upon it. The guards fell to the earth as dead men. When the women came to the tomb, they found neatly folded linens, but the Lord was gone!

Following the resurrection, Jesus met many times with His followers. His glorious voice spoke again and again, giving them the courage to continue in His way.

How strange this story is. The Gospel of Matthew reveals the fact that the Jewish leaders bribed the soldiers to lie about what happened that morning. Some silver probably found its way to Pilate's hands also, since the priests assured the soldiers they'd take care of the governor. The chief priests spread the story among all the people that Christ's followers had stolen His body and pretended He'd risen from the dead. I wonder how many really believed this explanation.

Following the crucifixion, the Bible describes a group of utterly demoralized apostles. "What's the use?" was the attitude of the moment. Depression and disillusionment prevailed.

Then came the resurrection. Jesus spent forty days with His disciples. They conducted a ten-day prayer meeting after His ascension to be with the Father.

The Day of Pentecost, fifty days after the resurrection, found them filled with courage and determination. The frightened, denying Peter was transformed into a brave soldier of Christ as he preached the sermon establishing the church. Gone was all doubt and estrangement. Those men went out and turned the world upside down for their Lord. They died bravely for the same Savior they'd deserted a short time before. Men don't act like that for a myth. The instinct of self-preservation is too great. That was a powerful, life-changing fifty days!

The fact is they'd finally learned their lesson. No force holds God! The life of Jesus exemplified this all the way through. Herod tried to destroy the infant Jesus. His strength failed next to God's power of discerning his evil intentions. Diseases of all kinds responded to Christ's touch. The winds and the waves obeyed His commands.

Finally, the strength of God was pitted against the force of the Roman Empire. The guards, the seal, the stone—all became toys in the power of the living God. Even the natural force of death itself failed to hold God's Son in its clutches. He arose!

The apostles seemed so slow in comprehension. We often feel they should have understood what He tried to teach long before the cross, the grave, and the resurrection. The fact remains that they didn't. But when it finally got through to them, they never failed Him again.

How's our comprehension? How's our spiritual quotient? Do we fly all directions at once because we neglect to reach out for God's power in our lives? How much do we really believe?

No force holds God! But we can limit His power in our own lives by refusal to trust Him. We can hamper His effectiveness with us by ignoring Him. The choice of harnessing this power in our lives is still ours.

Gracious heavenly Father, we're so thankful for Your tremendous functioning power in our universe. We're grateful to be able to worship a living Christ. We praise You that His life, death, and resurrection surpass all political and material power. Help us open our lives to You so that Your power will work through us to win people for Christ. In His name, amen.